DATE DUE

First Facts®

The Solar System

Revised and Updated

Saturn

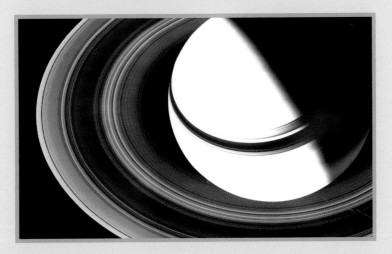

by Adele Richardson

Consultant:
Stephen J. Kortenkamp, PhD
Research Scientist
Planetary Science Institute, Tucson, Arizona

Capstone
press®
Mankato, Minnesota

First Facts is published by Capstone Press,
151 Good Counsel Drive, P.O. Box 669, Mankato, Minnesota 56002.
www.capstonepress.com

Library of Congress Cataloging-in-Publication Data
Richardson, Adele, 1966–
    Saturn / by Adele Richardson.—Rev. and updated.
    p. cm.—(First facts. The Solar system)
    Includes bibliographical references and index.
    ISBN-13: 978-1-4296-0728-5 (hardcover)
    ISBN-10: 1-4296-0728-9 (hardcover)
    1. Saturn (Planet)—Juvenile literature. I. Title. II. Series.
QB671.R54 2008
523.46—dc22   2007003536

Summary: Discusses the orbit, atmosphere, and exploration of the planet Saturn.

Editorial Credits
Christopher Harbo, editor; Juliette Peters, designer and illustrator; Jo Miller, photo researcher;
    Scott Thoms, photo editor

Photo Credits
NASA/JPL/Space Science Institute, 1, 9, 15
Photodisc, 4, planet images within illustrations and chart, 6–7, 11, 13, 19, 20, 21
Photo Researchers Inc./Science Photo Library/Detlav Van Ravenswaay, cover
Space Images/NASA/JPL, 5, 14, 17; STScl, 8, 16

1 2 3 4 5 6 12 11 10 09 08 07

Table of Contents

Voyager 1 and Saturn

In 1980, *Voyager 1* flew by Saturn.
The spacecraft took pictures of the giant
planet. The pictures showed a world
made of gases and ice. In some of the
pictures, scientists found moons they
had never seen before.

Fast Facts about Saturn

Diameter: 74,900 miles (120,540 kilometers)
Average Distance from Sun: 888 million miles
(1,429 million kilometers)
Average Temperature (cloud top): minus 285 degrees Fahrenheit
(minus 176 degrees Celsius)
Length of Day: 10 hours, 45 minutes
Length of Year: 29 Earth years, 6 months
Moons: at least 33
Rings: 7 ring groups, each made up of thousands of smaller rings

The Solar System

Saturn is the sixth planet from the Sun. It is one of the gas giants, along with Jupiter, Uranus, and Neptune. The four planets closest to the Sun are made of rock. They are Mercury, Venus, Earth, and Mars.

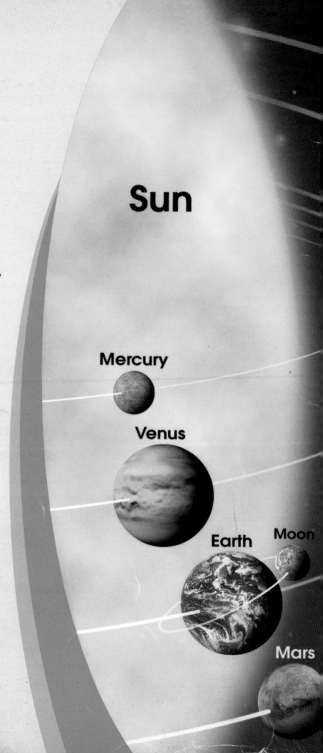

Sun

Mercury

Venus

Earth

Moon

Mars

Jupiter

Saturn

Uranus

Neptune

7

Saturn's Atmosphere

Saturn has a thick, cloudy **atmosphere**. An atmosphere is a layer of gases that surrounds a planet. Saturn's atmosphere is mostly **hydrogen** gas.

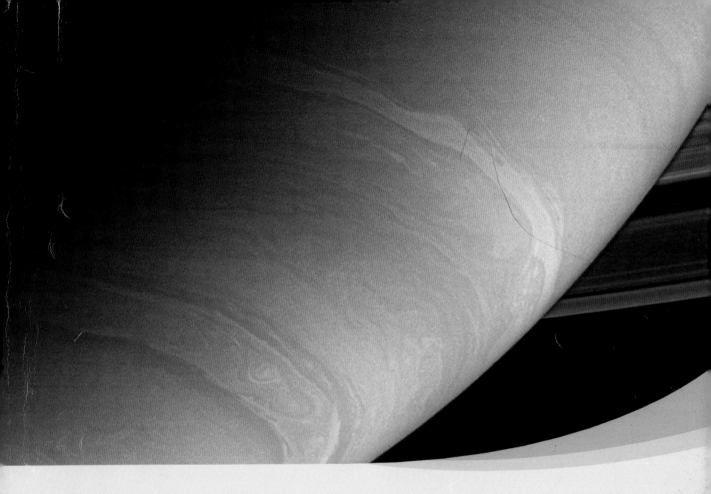

Clouds move quickly in Saturn's atmosphere. The planet has very strong winds. They can blow up to 1,100 miles (1,770 kilometers) per hour.

Saturn's Makeup

Saturn doesn't really have a surface. Its thick atmosphere pushes down toward the center of the planet. This pushing force is called **pressure**. Gases in Saturn's lower atmosphere become thick, like syrup. Saturn has a **core** of rock and ice at its center.

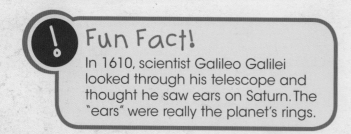

Fun Fact!
In 1610, scientist Galileo Galilei looked through his telescope and thought he saw ears on Saturn. The "ears" were really the planet's rings.

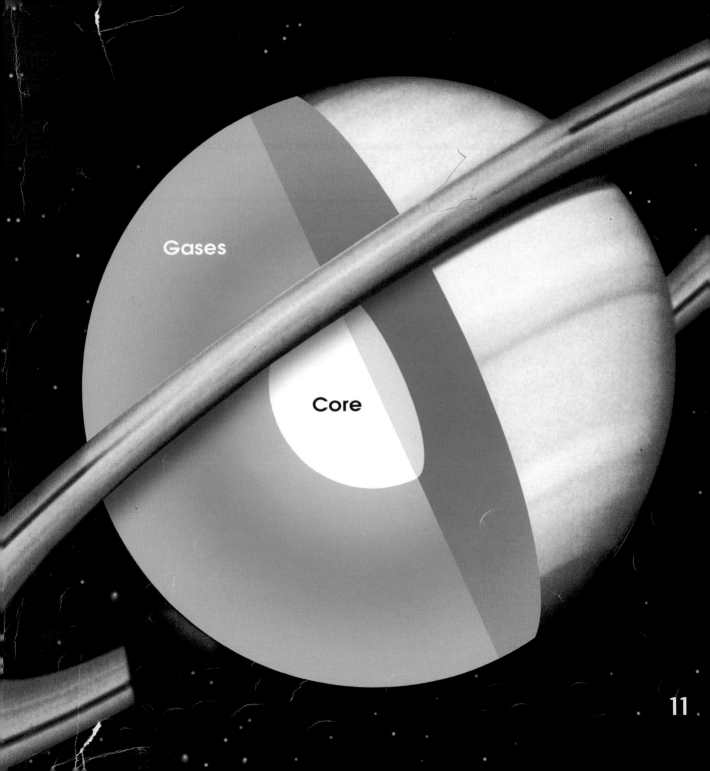

How Saturn Moves

Saturn spins quickly on its **axis** as it moves around the Sun. The planet completes one spin every 10 hours and 45 minutes. Saturn circles the Sun very slowly. The planet takes 29 Earth years and 6 months to circle the Sun.

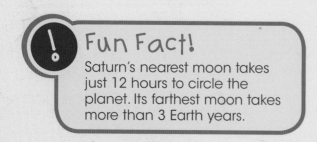

Fun Fact!

Saturn's nearest moon takes just 12 hours to circle the planet. Its farthest moon takes more than 3 Earth years.

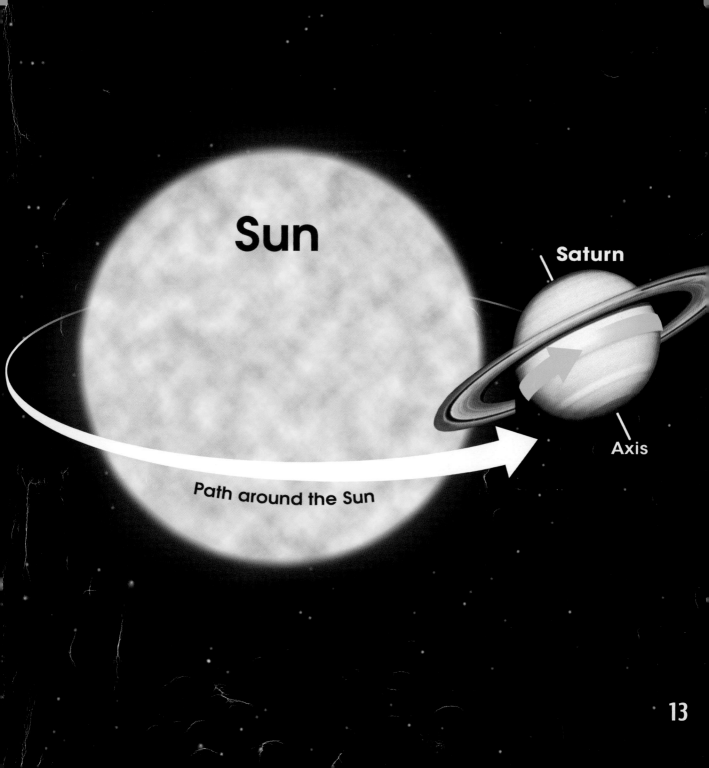

Sun

Saturn

Axis

Path around the Sun

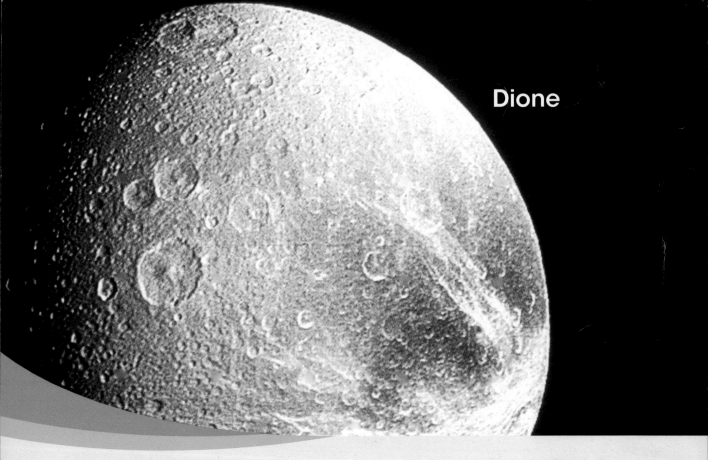

Dione

Moons and Rings

Saturn has at least 33 moons.
Saturn's moon Dione is covered with
craters. Titan is Saturn's largest moon.
It is bigger than the planet Mercury.

Saturn has seven large rings. These rings are made up of thousands of smaller rings called ringlets. Scientists think the rings are made mostly of ice.

Studying Saturn

People can see Saturn in the night sky. A **telescope** is needed to see the rings. Scientists use large telescopes to take good, clear pictures of Saturn.

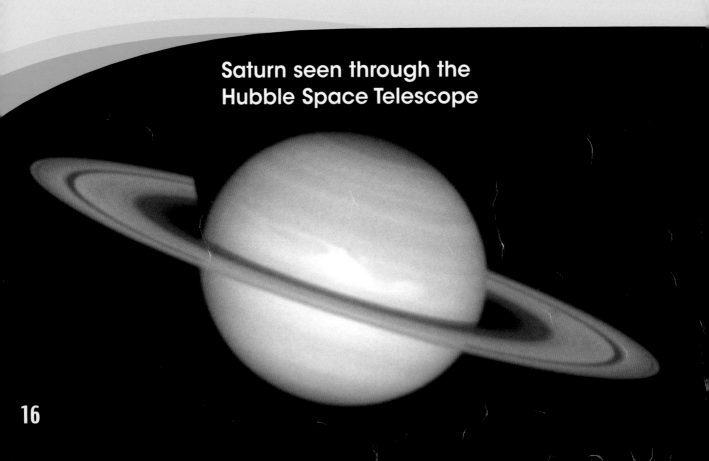

Saturn seen through the Hubble Space Telescope

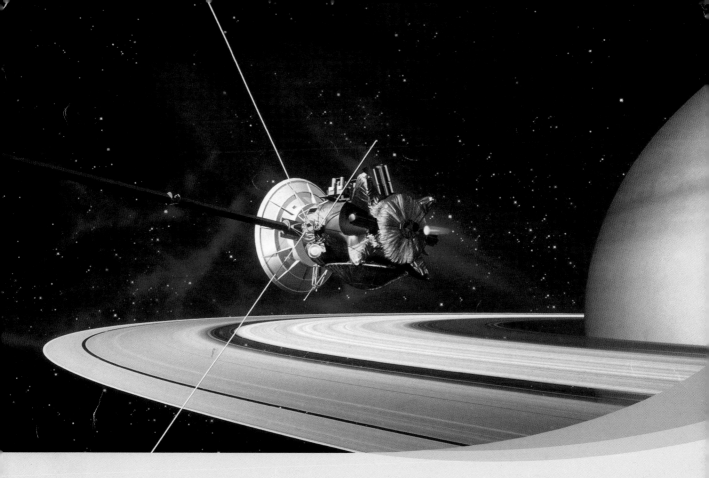

Scientists also use spacecraft to study Saturn. In 2004, the *Cassini* spacecraft reached Saturn. *Cassini* is studying the planet's rings, atmosphere, and moons.

Comparing Saturn to Earth

Saturn and Earth are very different. Earth is made of rock. Saturn is made of gases and ice. People could not breathe the gases on Saturn. High pressure would crush any spacecraft that entered the planet's atmosphere.

! Fun Fact!
Saturn's giant moon Titan has an atmosphere that is thicker and cloudier than Earth's atmosphere.

Size Comparison

Saturn

Earth

Amazing but True!

Would it sink or would it float? Saturn is the second largest planet in the solar system. But the planet is fluffy, like a giant cotton ball. If someone found a tub of water large enough to hold it, Saturn would float.

Planet Comparison Chart

Planet	Size Rank (1=largest)	Made Of	1 Trip Around the Sun (Earth Time)
Mercury	8	rock	88 days
Venus	6	rock	225 days
Earth	5	rock	365 days, 6 hours
Mars	7	rock	687 days
Jupiter	1	gases and ice	11 years, 11 months
Saturn	2	gases and ice	29 years, 6 months
Uranus	3	gases and ice	84 years
Neptune	4	gases and ice	164 years, 10 months

Glossary

atmosphere (AT-muhss-feehr)—the mixture of gases that surrounds some planets and moons

axis (AK-siss)—an imaginary line that runs through the middle of a planet; a planet spins on its axis.

core (KOR)—the inner part of a planet that is made of metal or rock

crater (KRAY-tur)—a hole made when an asteroid or a large piece of rock crashes into a planet or moon

hydrogen (HYE-druh-juhn)—a colorless gas that is lighter than air and burns easily

pressure (PRESH-ur)—the force produced by pressing on something

telescope (TEL-uh-skope)—an instrument that makes faraway objects appear larger and closer

Read More

Kortenkamp, Steve. *Why Isn't Pluto a Planet?: A Book about Planets.* First Facts: Why in the World? Mankato, Minn.: Capstone Press, 2007.

Orme, Helen, and David Orme. *Let's Explore Saturn.* Space Launch! Milwaukee: Gareth Stevens, 2007.

Taylor-Butler, Christine. *Saturn.* Scholastic News Nonfiction Readers. New York: Children's Press, 2007.

Internet Sites

FactHound offers a safe, fun way to find Internet sites related to this book. All of the sites on FactHound have been researched by our staff.

Here's how:
1. Visit *www.facthound.com*
2. Choose your grade level.
3. Type in this book ID **1429607289** for age-appropriate sites. You may also browse subjects by clicking on letters, or by clicking on pictures and words.
4. Click on the **Fetch It** button.

FactHound will fetch the best sites for you!

Index